Michael grew up in Wisconsin. He is a U.S. Navy veteran and a graduate of the University of Wisconsin. Michael currently resides in Florida with his wife.

For my wife, my family, and for old friends.

Michael Gautz

THE QUITTER

AUSTIN MACAULEY PUBLISHERS™

LONDON • CAMBRIDGE • NEW YORK • SHARJAH

Ordering Information
Quantity sales: Special discounts are available on quantity purchases by corporations, associations, and others. For details, contact the publisher at the address below.

Publisher's Cataloging-in-Publication data
Gautz, Michael
The Quitter

ISBN 9781685623302 (Paperback)
ISBN 9781685623319 (ePub e-book)

Library of Congress Control Number: 2023904532

www.austinmacauley.com/us

First Published 2023
Austin Macauley Publishers LLC
40 Wall Street, 33rd Floor, Suite 3302
New York, NY 10005
USA

mail-usa@austinmacauley.com
+1 (646) 5125767

Introduction

When Mike walked out of the poker room, he was mad and talking to himself. It was 2 O'clock in the morning and as he headed towards his car, he was the only person in the parking lot. He had spent the whole evening playing poker and he had lost $800. Mike hoped that when he arrived at home that his wife would be asleep. She was sitting on the couch watching a movie when he walked into the house and he knew that she would question him about losing money. Mike didn't give her a chance to talk though, he started right in making conversation. "I can never win when I go there," he said. "I play good, solid poker and I still can't win."

His wife just sat there looking at him and he continued. "I had a pair of kings and the other guy had a pair of Aces." "I had a straight and the other guy rivered a flush!" "All day long I had the second-best hand and all that did have cost me money. I am tired of being ripped off!" Mike hollered. He then made a promise to his wife. "I quit, no more poker for me," he said. "Oh I have heard that before," his wife said, "how many times are you going to quit?" "You are just a quitter," she told him. "Yes, I am a quitter," Mike thought to himself, *I have always been a quitter.*

Football

Mike grew up in Wisconsin, the home of the Packers. He was born in 1960 and he remembers watching them every Sunday on his grandfather's television. Those were the glory years of Lombardi, Starr, and Nitschke. Mike remembers watching the first two super bowls, the Packers winning them easily. So Mike grew up loving football and wanting to be a football player like Ray Nitschke. Number 66 was his favorite player because he looked mean, he was tough and he tackled hard. Mike liked the way Nitschke's face looked at the end of a game, dirty, a tooth missing in the front, a crooked nose, and a big smile always on his face after every game.

Mike skipped a grade in school going from the second grade to the fourth grade because he had some smarts and because he was quick-witted. He remembers evenings with his mother helping him with math flashcards. Two times two is four, four times four is 16. Mike could holler out the answers faster than any of the other students. Later in life, he would sometimes be called a wise-ass but for now, he was just a bit ahead of his class. Mike didn't realize it at the time but skipping a grade made him a year younger than his classmates. All of the other boys were a year bigger and faster than he was. It would remain that way all the rest of his school years, Mike would almost always find himself up against athletes older, bigger, and stronger than himself.

Mike started playing football in some of the neighborhood games. These games were tackled football with no equipment on. The older players let Mike play to even up the sides and he was usually the last person picked to play. But Mike didn't mind as he was in the game and he would give it his best. After a while, some of the older boys took a liking to Mike because of the way he played. He was a competitor and he had courage. He didn't run away when they came running at him. He would stand his ground, take a hit and make the tackle. Mike loved playing this game, he was learning from the older players and he was getting better. He was also being accepted by the older boys but only on the field. Once the game was over the older boys would go their way and Mike would go his. Word got around the school playground and a few times Mike was picked to play in the games at recess. One of the older boys playing a quarterback who knew Mike would wait until nobody was paying attention to Mike and then drill him a pass right in the chest for a touchdown. There was no way that Mike was going to drop the ball, he knew that the pressure was on him and he wanted to play. So he caught every pass that was thrown to him and he stuck his face in the middle of every tackle that came his way.

When Mike was in the sixth grade a friend of his family invited him to play football on a Catholic School team. The team had players on it from the sixth to the eighth grade. Once again Mike would be the youngest player on the team but he was thrilled to be playing organized ball. Mike didn't get to play much, mostly standing around on the sidelines wondering if there were better things to be doing on a Saturday afternoon. The few times that he did get in the games were against weaker teams when the score had already been run-up. But when Mike played, he loved it and he was good. He had two interceptions in the two games he played in and he made many tackles for the second-string defense. His team won the Catholic School championship that year and before the season was over, they played an exhibition game against the YMCA league champions. Mike stood on the sideline for most of the game as usual. The other team had a big strong running back who was tearing up the field and hitting everybody hard.

Finally, towards the end of the game, the coach put Mike in for one play, his only play of the game. He was on the kick-off team and was in his position of players spread out across the field. His Teammate kicked the ball and Mike ran up the field. The big strong running back from the other team caught the ball and started running straight at Mike, the youngest player on the field. Mike got ready for the upcoming collision and dared not turn away. The running back slammed right into him like a locomotive ramming a cow. Mike just held out his arms, took the blow, and fell to his back. But the running back also fell landing on top of Mike who had made the tackle. Mike got up slowly and he felt weak. It was the hardest hit he had ever taken. But he just trotted off of the field like nothing had happened, he couldn't show the others the pain he was in. That was the only year Mike played for that team.

Between the sixth and the eighth grades, Mike played a few games for a YMCA team. The problem with the YMCA was that they tried to evenly distribute the good and the bad players on different teams. As Mike was considered as a pretty good player he was placed on a bad team. Mike wasn't a ball-handler, he played mostly defense. His coach tried playing him at wide receiver because he could catch the ball, but the quarterback was never able to get the ball out to him. They did not win a game all year.

Like most of the kids at his public school, Mike waited anxiously to be eligible to play on the ninth-grade team. This was the only team his school had and it was the year before high school ball. Mike was still one year younger than his teammates. He practiced most of the summer with the team getting ready for the opening day of school and the first game. As usual, Mike spent most of his time on the sidelines watching and waiting for his chance. Occasionally the coach put him in with the second-string defense and he played middle linebacker. Mike soon realized that most of the boys were bigger and faster than him but he could tackle. Soon he was playing in the practices on a regular basis and he was loving it. Those hard summer workouts were becoming fun as he clashed helmets and became a force on the defense. As the season opener neared the team played a scrimmage game against a nearby school. Mike did not start the game but played most of the second half at linebacker. He almost had an interception as a batted pass fell just in front of him as he dove to try and catch the ball. He made a few tackles and felt that it was a good day. He was ready for the season to begin.

And then something happened. Something Mike would never forget. A man from the local newspaper office came to Mike's house and offered him a job as a paperboy delivering newspapers. Of course, if he accepted the job, he would have to quit playing football as the job was every day. Mike thought briefly about the offer of money and decided to take the job.

"Are you sure you want to quit playing football?" Mike's mother asked him, "Yesterday football was all you wanted to do." But Mike said yes, he was sure. His goals had changed. Now he wanted to work and to make some money. Little did he know what professional football players would be making in the near future.

That was the end of Mike's football playing days. The end of his first passion in life. The team that he quit went undefeated that year, public school champions. Most of the players went on to play high school ball but not Mike. The summer before the high school season opened all of the players were invited to the gym to work out daily in the weight room. "I would rather deliver newspapers than spend my whole summer in a smelly weight room," Mike said. And that is what he did.

Mike did play some football once a week with friends but it was not an organized game. They played the old games of no equipment football. They would often take cigarette breaks during the game. Some of the guys were good players but none of them played on the school team. Most of them ended up as factory workers.

Basketball

When Mike started high school, he was no longer an athlete. He began to hang around with the boys outside of school. He started smoking cigarettes and drinking beer. He also tried some marijuana when he could afford it. Those were fun-filled days for Mike, skipping classes, smoking, drinking, and laughing with friends. Mike occasionally went to school but he didn't go to classes. He was bored with mathematics, physics, and biology. Mike was a smart kid having skipped a grade but he never thought that he would go to college. Only the smartest guys in the class would be doctors, only the rich kids would go to college or so Mike thought. Mike thought that he would probably end up as a factory worker like his father. When Mike did go to school, he didn't go to the classroom but he headed straight for the gymnasium. He was in the gym almost every day for hours at a time. This is where Mike found his next passion: Basketball.

Mike actually started playing basketball when he was in the sixth grade. The same gentleman who was the Catholic school football coach was also the eighth-grade basketball coach. The coach talked with the fifth-grade coach who let Mike join the team. As Mike had skipped a grade, he was actually the same age as the fifth graders. He also was attending a public school. But in those years, it wasn't a big deal and Mike didn't look big enough or good enough for anyone to take notice of him. There was one player on Mike's team who was an outstanding player for a fifth-grader. His name was John and his father was the coach. John could shoot and he could score. John led the league in points scored that year, and he led the team to an 11 win and one loss season. Mike played well averaging six to eight points a game but with John, as the main offensive weapon, Mike became a defensive player. No matter which team they played Mike always wanted to guard their best player. St Johns had a star player who later played high school ball. During their game, Mike shut him down by not allowing him to get open for a pass. St Lucy had a guard who was supposed to be quick and a shooter. During their game, Mike was in his face the whole game keeping him 30 feet away from the basket. He never got off a shot. Meanwhile, John kept scoring points and ringing up victories for his team.

The end of the season saw Mike's team tied with St Stan's at 10 wins and one loss. There would be a playoff game for the championship. St Stan's was reported to have some good players, mainly their guards who could shoot from the outside.

The one-game playoff started off as usual with John's repeated scoring putting Mike's team in the lead. Then in the second half, something unusual happened as John got into foul trouble and ended up fouling out midway through the second half. John had to spend the rest of the championship game on the bench. Some of the players panicked but Mike didn't. He knew what to do. He would try and waste as much time as possible and hold on to the lead. So when he got the ball Mike didn't run up the court he walked. When the other team had the ball he stuck to the ball-handling guard closely making them waste as much time as possible trying to get off a pass or a shot. And the plan worked. Mike's team held on to the lead and won the championship.

The next week they held a banquet for all of the players and each team was given *a* most valuable player trophy. Mike heard the coaches discussing who should get his team's trophy. One coach said, "Hell John should get the trophy, those guys did nothing after he was out of the game." John did get the most valuable player trophy. Mike knew that John deserved it. But Mike also knew that he had played great defense all year and had helped to win the championship game by holding off the other team.

As with the football team, that was the only year Mike played for the Catholic school. Two championships, football, and basketball in the same year.

Mike played a bit of basketball in the seventh grade on the public-school team. But he was back with the older boys now, and it was easy to see the difference. Every boy was a foot taller than Mike and they could run faster. So Mike got bored, quit the team, and only played intramural ball once a week. Mike didn't play much basketball for the next couple of years after that as nobody in his neighborhood wanted to play. Most of the boys in that part of town played baseball and Mike didn't like baseball.

Then Mike hit high school age and saw the big gymnasium with the plexiglass backboards all around the gym. As mentioned around this time Mike had become bored with school. He spent most of his time lounging around outside of the school wondering what he was going to do with himself. The gym was open to anybody during the midday hours and Mike began to go there from time to time to shoot baskets. As the year went by Mike would be in the gym almost every day, playing basketball. He no longer evens went to any of his classes. The boys would play pick-up games, two against two, half-court. Mike had a friend named Dan and they played pretty well together. Mike could shoot the ball. After hours and hours of practice, he could shoot from anywhere on the court and make it.

But Mike didn't try out for the school team. He didn't like school and the school didn't like him. He was always in trouble for skipping classes or smoking on school property. The coaches wouldn't let anyone on their team who smoked.

The players on the high school team were also a lot bigger than Mike. Some of them played football and basketball during different seasons. The center for the basketball team was 6 feet 11 inches tall and weighed about 250 pounds. There were also many black players on the team.

Mike had not seen many black people growing up. There were none in his school until he was in the seventh grade. He doesn't remember playing against any black players in the catholic league. But high school was a mixture of black and white people and Mike began to see the way they played the game. They ran up and down the court playing full-court, not half. They usually didn't pass the ball but just ran down the court and took a shot. These were the years of the run and gun style of basketball. Mike started watching a lot of basketball on the television and kept going to the gym. But he knew that he was not as good as the players on the varsity team.

About this time Mike's mother decided to get remarried and move to Indiana. Mike had no choice but to go along. He also became interested in the prospect of playing Indiana basketball. This would be a fresh start for Mike. He could go to school, go by the rules, and maybe even try out for the team. So Mike spent the summer playing in pick-up games with his new neighbors. When the school year started, he went to classes and he did his homework. He also resumed going to the gym every day when it was open. The boys he played against were not really that good but Mike knew that these were not the varsity players. The best players at the school were still playing on the football team. Once football season ended, they would return to the basketball court. That is how it worked in those northern states.

So when the first team tryouts began all of the last year's players were there, including the football players. Mike looked around and he realized that the team members had probably already been decided upon. The coach knew them all by name, and they all knew each other. The team practiced some lay-up drills and then had a short scrimmage. The coach pointed at Mike and he joined in. Mike immediately went to defense on the guard who was one of the best players on the team. They ran up and down the floor a few times and Mike scored twice, once being on a nice jump shot from the free-throw circle. But Mike knew he was an outsider and not wanted. The coach didn't even know his name, how could he get on the roster? So Mike quit the team after the first day of practice without even giving it a chance. Better to quit now as I would probably just sit on the bench all season anyway is what Mike thought.

Mike even quit going to school again even though he had a B average at his new school. He was bored with school and wanted to find a job. He missed his hometown and the friends of the past but he couldn't go back. Now he was a high school dropout.

Friends

Mike had a lot of friends when he was growing up. Now he doesn't have any. When he was younger there was a group of boys almost his age living in his neighborhood. They would walk to school together almost every day. Mike always invited his friends to his birthday parties. One year all of the boys went to see the Coast Guard station together.

Mike knew most of these boys all the way through his high school years. Most of his neighborhood friends were not athletes. The boys did other things together. Mike's mother grew tomatoes in their backyard. Some nights just for fun the boys would raid the garden and then go out and throw tomatoes at the cars driving by on the busy street. In the winter they would throw snowballs. Another one of the boys' pastimes was called skitching. When a bus or a truck came past on a snowy road, the boys would grab onto the rear bumper and be pulled down the road a mile or two.

Most of the time the boys would just sit around outside in a nearby vacant field and smoke cigarettes. All of the boys started smoking at a young age. Mike remembers having to hide his pack of cigarettes from his parents outside the house and hopes that they didn't get wet. The boys also began playing cards together. Some nights they would play for pennies. They all sat around gambling and smoking at one of the boy's house. His mother was usually at work and didn't mind the boys in her house. At least they were not outside making trouble.

As the boys got a little older, they went to a few student parties together. Mike remembers one night he and his friends sat around together drinking a bottle of whiskey. When Mike went home and went to bed the whole room started spinning around in circles. The room kept on spinning until Mike finally threw up all over himself. The next day Mike told his friends about it. One boy said, "You know what, the same thing happened to me!"

Those were carefree days for Mike and the boys always had fun together. One night they all went to a Cub Scout carnival. Inside you had to buy tickets to play the games or to buy food. Towards the end of the evening, Mike quietly walked behind one of the ticket counters without being noticed. There he found a whole roll of unused tickets. Mike picked up the tickets and walked off as calmly as could be. Then he and his friends walked over to the hot dog stand and bought fifty hot dogs. They all went outside and Mike passed around the hot dogs. After the boys ate a few, they decided to have some fun and they started throwing hot dogs at each other. Hot dogs were flying at all of the people who were exiting the carnival.

As the boys reached high school age, they began to go their separate ways. The card games became less frequent. One of the boys became a construction worker with his dad's company. Another boy quit school and started working in a factory. Another one of his friends found a girlfriend and he spent all of his time with her. Mike went to the gym almost every day and quit seeing his friends.

Mike knew a lot of people then but they weren't really friends. They were more like acquaintances. Looking back on those times Mike thought, *I could have been a politician, all the people I knew.*

But after high school, Mike didn't have any close friends. He didn't have time for people. He knew the guys at the gym because he saw them almost every day. But he didn't know any of their last names. When the game was over Mike went his own way alone. He became a loner. He would read a few hours, go to work then go to bed.

Mike had basically quit trying to make friends. As he grew into his adult years, he kept more and more to himself. He lived alone. He went out to eat by himself. He went out to the bar by himself. Mike remembers many nights just standing alone in the singles bar looking at people and having a drink. He moved far away from his hometown and most of those young people he never saw again. In the new town that he had moved to he knew nobody. Mike wasn't much of a talker and he didn't have great interpersonal skills. It was hard for him to make friends. The place that Mike felt most comfortable was on the playing field or in the gymnasium. Mike rarely talked to anybody. Even some of the people at work told him that he was too quiet. This annoyed Mike even more. He had become a quiet, serious person and he wanted to be left alone. He didn't have the patience or the desire to stand around talking about nothing important. Mike's aunt once told him, "You are as serious as a heart attack."

Mike even started to avoid people. Frequently he would go to the coffee shop and sit far away from the other people so he could read quietly. When he did talk to other people, he was short and abrupt. He couldn't relate to people on a casual basis as he thought that was a waste of time. Mike thought about getting himself a dog to keep him company. He decided against that as he had no desire to clean up crap off of the floor.

Mike knew he couldn't just quit interacting with other people although sometimes he wished that he could. He often wondered if he should become a monk. Then he could sit in a quiet place and read all day. Mike soon gave up on that idea as he realized that he wasn't holy enough.

Mike tried to relax and be more outgoing. He thought about his uncle who is a businessman. His uncle had many friends and was always smiling and talking to people. But Mike realized that his uncle was probably taught to act that way in business school and Mike just wasn't that way. Sometimes Mike would stand at work and listen to somebody talking about fantasy football even though Mike thought that to be a waste of time.

Then one night while Mike was eating alone in a restaurant, he met a new waitress. He liked her and started talking to her. She took a liking to Mike and they started dating. Now he has a friend he can talk to. He is glad he didn't become a monk.

Baseball, Golf, Tennis

Wisconsin is a seasonal state and so are its sports. In the summer people either play baseball, golf, or tennis. At some point in his life, Mike played all of them.

Mike never did like baseball very much. "You just stand there all day in the hot sun waiting for the ball to come your way and then you are under pressure to make the play," is what he thought. He played some baseball and softball because all of the other boys did. When Mike was in the sixth grade, he played on the school's eleven-inch softball team. Mike is a left-hander and he played the second base position. Mike was still the youngest amongst his schoolmates and the youngest player on the team. There were a couple of boys who had been set back in school and were older than anyone else on the team. They were the best players on the team and probably the best players in the league. The team finished first in their division that year with the two older boys leading the league in hitting. The league was divided into North and South divisions and Mike's team made it to the North Division championship game.

The game was close with only a one-run difference going into the final inning. The other team had a runner on first base. The next hitter hit a blooper pop fly ball just over the second base. Mike ran out after it into short center field. Because he was left-handed Mike was able to reach way out with his gloved right hand and make the catch. He then turned as fast as he could and threw the ball back to first base catching the runner off of the base for a double play. The next batter made the third out and Mike's team won the North division championship. The school received a huge trophy which is still in their display some forty years later. The fifth and sixth grades were Mike's glory years in sports. He was on championship teams in football, basketball, and softball.

Mike also played some little league baseball. He was a left-handed outfielder and pitcher. He had a strong arm and he could hit the ball. Once he hit a line drive over the left fielder's head and the ball went all of the way to the deep uncut grass at the edge of the field. When he was pitching Mike threw hard and wildly. He hit many players with the ball and scared some of the boys with his pitching.

But the sixth grade was the end of Mike's baseball playing. When he was much older, he played some games with an adult bar league team but he soon lost interest. He never really did like baseball and he quit going to the games.

Mike also started playing golf at an early age. The town they lived in had a few public golf courses Mike's uncle was a golfer and he bought Mike a set of clubs. The public courses had a summer pass plan for teenagers: all the golf you wanted to play all summer for $25. Mike got a pass and was at the golf course almost every day. He just kept walking the course and hitting the ball. He sometimes played 36 or 45 holes a day. It seems that whatever Mike did he wanted to do it well. He was a competitor. He wanted to show the other boys that he could play. He wanted to be the best. But Mike never took any golf lessons. He only had a basic understanding of the game. As he looked around, he saw other boys his same age shooting much better scores than him and they were winning the tournaments. One boy only a year older than Mike was already shooting at a par score level. He won the city championship every year. Mike read a book on golf fundamentals that really improved his game. But Mike knew that he would never be good enough. Besides golf and golf equipment are expensive. *Golf is a rich man's game,* Mike thought. And so after a few years, Mike quit golfing. The best he could score was in the high 70s.

Tennis was another game that Mike considered to be a rich man's game. The school Mike went to had some old beat-up tennis courts that were rarely used. The only time Mike remembers anyone using the courts was when they were playing dodge ball using the fenced-in area. The school did have a large brick wall with a line painted across it at about the height of a tennis net. Mike's grandmother would let him use her old tennis racquet. He would go over to that wall and bang the tennis ball against it for hours. Once again Mike never took any tennis lessons or had any formal training but he could hit the ball.

Some of the other kids, the rich kids belonged to country clubs. They had nice tennis courts to play on and their parents bought them nice equipment. They didn't associate with Mike. He didn't play on a country club court until he was college-aged. Mike enjoyed tennis but it wasn't his passion. He found a friend to hit balls with and they spent hours knocking them back and forth. It was a good exercise. But as Mike reached his high school and then his college years, he had to decide which sport he wanted to devote his time to. And Mike had chosen basketball. He still played tennis occasionally. He remembers a few times playing some tennis in the morning and then playing some basketball that same afternoon. The college tennis coach asked Mike if he was going to try out for their team. Mike said no. He knew that he wasn't good enough and he wanted to spend his time in the gym playing basketball. Mike also took a short trip to Florida for a spring break when he was in college. He went to a fancy resort near Tampa where you could pay for a day of tennis lessons. There he played and took lessons for a couple of days. He saw around him how good some of the players were. That's all they did was play tennis. They talked about how the professionals sometimes played here. Mike knew he would never get to that level and he quit playing tennis.

Military

So after Mike quite high school he sat around at his parents' house wondering what to do with himself. He couldn't get a decent job because he wasn't a high school graduate. He didn't have a car to drive. Sometimes he drove his sister's car that had a stick shift. One night after he was out drinking, he lost control of his sister's car in the snow and rammed it into a telephone pole. He rarely had money to go out on the weekends. Most of Mike's friends were still going to school and would graduate. Mike soon lost touch with most of them. He even knew a couple of guys who were not as smart as him who would soon be graduating.

One day Mike's uncle came over and saw Mike sitting on the couch doing nothing. "Why don't you join the Navy?" he said. "You will get paid and you can do some traveling." That is just what Mike needed. It would be a good way to get out of this town for a while. So his uncle took him over to the local recruiters' office where Mike sat for a couple of hours taking an entrance examination. Mike had no trouble passing the exam. After he had finished the recruiter asked him what kind of job he wanted to do or what he wanted to be. Mike had no idea what he wanted to be and he told the guy so. Little did Mike know but that would be his first mistake in the Navy, not choosing the job he wanted.

So Mike hopped on a plane for San Diego going to boot camp and was happy to be leaving his bad days behind him. He had heard that boot camp was tough and that he had to be in good physical shape but Mike wasn't worried. He had been doing a lot of running lately and he even decided to quit smoking. Boot camp turned out to be monotonous. Everyone just got up early and spent the day marching around from place to place. Mike got his hair cut, got his shots, and got his teeth checked all for free. The most interesting day of boot camp was the firefighting training. They marched everyone into a smoke-filled room. Mike could not see the guy next to him it was so smoky. Everyone held hands with the guy next to them and didn't dare let go. Nobody wanted to get lost in there. The second most interesting day at boot camp was when the recruits were given lectures on venereal disease and low women. "You know," Mike told the guy next to him, "The first thing I am going to do when I get out of here is to go and find me one of those low women." They both laughed.

After Mike graduated boot camp, they sent him to Great Lakes Illinois to a ten-week school. Back at Great Lakes, Mike would again be back in the cold weather. He wished he were back in San Diego. At the time the Navy had a needs list for certain jobs. These jobs were in high need because nobody wanted to do that kind of work. This is exactly where they put Mike. He walked around the school for ten weeks looking at steam pipes over his head and not really knowing what he was doing. His shift time sometimes varied and he often found himself walking around looking at pipes in the middle of the night. But Mike didn't care. He was getting a paycheck every two weeks and he had money in his pocket.

Finally, Mike finished school and was headed for his assigned ship. He still didn't really know what his work was going to be. Mike was headed for Pearl Harbor Hawaii, a place he had always wanted to see. When Mike arrived at his ship the first thing, they did was give him the dirtiest, nastiest job they could find for him, cleaning the latrine. There had been a recent ship inspection and the bathrooms had received bad marks for cleanliness. Mike was a good worker. He always took pride in his work. He was in that bathroom for weeks polishing and shining the pipes. "Just like the pipes at the school, they sent me to." Mike chuckled to himself. When someone wanted to use the bathroom Mike kept an eye out so that the guy would not piss on the floor or something. Soon the inspectors came around and reported that, "The latrine showed much improvement." The ship leaders sent Mike along to his next Navy job, washing dishes.

The cooks on board the ship were all Filipinos and they cooked in giant pots which Mike had to clean every day. Mike spent his entire day from early before breakfast until late after dinner cleaning pots and pans. For the first few weeks of this Mike didn't mind. He was happy just to have a job and be away from home. When Mike could get a day off, he would follow some of the other sailors to Hotel Street. This area of Hawaii was full of bars and bar girls. All of the sailors would sit around buying the girls expensive drinks. Mike even met a nice girl on Hotel Street whom he took a liking to. She worked in one of the bars at night and

Mike went to see her every payday. She said her name was Venus and she was a slim, petite Hawaiian girl. Mike just wanted to be with one girl and he chose Venus over all of the other girls whenever he visited.

But Mike was soon becoming unhappy with life in the Navy. One of the problems in the military is that everyone wants to be the boss and nobody wants to do the work. Everyone kept telling Mike what to do and giving him the worst jobs to do. Mike tried to make the best of his time and tried to improve himself. He took a high school English class and then passed his GED exam. Now he was a high school graduate. Next, he completed a college-level history course which was offered while onboard the ship. He even worked on some Navy aircraft maintenance courses. It turned out though that Mike was color blind and he wasn't accepted to do that work.

So Mike was still given the worst jobs and he became more and more frustrated. His next job was to be the messenger of the watch. His main task was to go around the ship in the middle of the night waking up sailors for their watch. He remembers one guy in particular, a chief petty officer. Mike would have to go back to his bunk three or four times to get him out of bed. *How the hell did this guy ever become a chief?* Mike thought. Mike became more and more annoyed with his job and he began to argue and fight with people.

One time the ship stopped in Hong Kong. At that time the island was still ruled by the British. Mike was allowed a day off. He went outside near the ship to catch a cab. He then asked the cab driver to take him to a bar that the other sailors had mentioned. After he was in the cab for about fifteen minutes, he noticed passing by a building they had already passed before. He started arguing with the cab driver. "What the hell are you doing, driving around in circles to charge a higher fare?" "We have already been down this street, stop the cab now!" Mike screamed.

The cab driver stopped and as Mike got out the driver said, "I want twenty dollars American now."

"That's ridiculous," yelled Mike, "All you did was drive back to the same street, where is the bar?"

"Over there you must walk," said the driver.

Mike knew he was being ripped off but what could he do? So Mike rolled up a twenty-dollar bill in his fist and gave it to the driver, punching him right in the stomach. The driver toppled over and Mike walked away. He eventually found the bar about a mile away and sat down and had a few drinks.

When Mike returned to the ship he was in big trouble. The cab driver had reported the incident to the police and they were looking for Mike. He was restricted to the ship and the next day he was to appear in a Hong Kong court.

Mike went to the court in his Navy uniform accompanied by an officer. They were also followed by a military policeman with a gun. "What do they think, am I going to run away in Hong Kong?" Mike asked. They sat down in the courtroom and the lawyers started talking to each other. Finally, the cab driver who was at the other table stood up and lifted up his shirt. His whole abdomen was covered by a large gauze dressing.

"What is this nonsense?" Mike asked his lawyer. The judge looked at the cab driver and knew that he was faking an injury. But what could they do? They had to make a deal.

So the judge looked at the cab driver and said, "500 dollars American do you take it or not?"

The cabbies lawyer said, "Yes your honor, and that was that."

So Mike went back to the ship. He was told the 500 dollars would be taken out of his pay so he would be working for nothing. He was also told that in his military record it would be noted that he had caused an international incident.

Mike was getting tired of being bossed around. He was tired of having to stay on board the ship and do lousy jobs when everyone else was walking off of the ship for liberty.

One day Mike was getting some rest in his bunk. One of the guys whom Mike didn't like anyway was near him and playing his music too loud. Mike asked him to turn the music down. The guy refused, it was his time off and he was going to do as he pleased. Mike went over to the guy and started arguing. The arguing soon became a fight. Mike and the other guy were soon throwing punches. Soon two of the higher-ranking petty officers were trying to break up the fight. Mike was tough and in good shape and he continued to fight all three of them.

So, Mike ended up being arrested and thrown in the military jail with three counts of assault against him. *So much for military justice,* Mike thought. After Mike returned to the ship he was again put on restriction and he couldn't leave the ship. And again they took away half of his pay as a penalty. Now Mike was really mad. They were repeatedly making him do lousy work for no pay. They were making him stay on the ship all of the time and he couldn't go and see his friend Venus.

Things were getting worse and worse for Mike. He was mad at everyone around him. Finally one day he requested to have a talk with the captain of the ship. The captain told him that he might be discharged from the Navy. Mike told the captain, "That is OK with me, I quit, I want to find a real job." The captain was happy to comply with Mike and the paperwork started for his discharge.

They sent Mike to live in a barracks onshore until his discharge papers were completed. He attended a hearing and he had an appointed military lawyer on his side who turned out to be useless. Mike was actually happier at the barracks. His job was cleaning the gymnasium, a place Mike liked to be at. He played some basketball on his days off. He was allowed to walk around outside and to walk to and from the mess hall where they had great food. There Mike would eat two or three desserts and he didn't have to worry about doing the dishes. He was even allowed to leave the base and see Venus when he had some money. They had a good friendship. She took Mike to her apartment some days where they sat and talked for hours.

Finally, Mike's discharge papers came in and he was going back home to Wisconsin. He couldn't stay in Hawaii, what would he do there? He said goodbye to Venus and they were both sad that he had to leave.

So Mike had quit going to school twice. He had quit trying to be what he wanted to be the most, an athlete. He had quit and been thrown out of the Navy which was his paying job. He had quit and left his only friend behind. Just what would he do with himself now?

Smoking, Drinking, Drugs

Mike started smoking when he was a teenager. His mother smoked and he would sometimes steal some of her cigarettes. Once he had a job in a gas station and all of the mechanics smoked. Everyone walked around all day with a butt hanging from their mouth. It was the thing to do. When Mike was in high school, he would skip his classes and sit outside across the street from the school smoking. He was bored with school and it gave him a chance to meet other people. Mike began to smoke more and more, about a half of a pack per day. Back then cigarettes were cheap. He also had a friend who worked at a convenience store and he could get them at a discount. All of the neighborhood boys would sit around all day smoking.

Mike also began to drink alcohol when he was about fifteen years old. The legal age for drinking in Wisconsin was 18. Mike had a friend who was a big fellow and who played on the football team. His friend was a heavy drinker. Sometimes he would take Mike to the bar with him. The bar owner didn't take notice of the underage drinkers because he was making money. In Wisconsin, there is a bar on almost every corner. Some of them had an upstairs apartment where the owner lived. During the long, cold winters the bar was where everyone usually spent their time at night.

Mike's friend would sometimes pick him up in his car in the morning on the way to school. They would usually each drink a couple of cans of beer before school. Mike would then sit outside all morning waiting for the gym to open. The teachers and the coaches at the school all knew who the smokers were and they would not allow them on their teams.

About this time Mike found a job working in a liquor store as a handler. After work, all of the workers would sit down and have a drink before going home. Mike would have a beer. One day at work Mike decided to have some fun. Behind the store, the railroad tracks ran back towards town. One evening after work Mike grabbed a case of apple wine and hid it behind the store in the tall grass. When he was finished working, he picked up the case of wine and walked down the railroad tracks until he came to a junkyard near the end of the tracks. There he met some of his friends. They spent the whole evening sitting in an old school bus drinking wine and having a good time.

Another night Mike went to a party at a friend's house. Mike drank liquor all night long. Then he went outside and fell asleep on his friend's front lawn. When he woke up it was morning and there were cars driving past on the road. Mike got up and walked home like it was no big deal.

Mike's father was an alcoholic. He wasted his life sitting around drinking beer and not going to work. Mike's drinking began to get him in trouble. His uncle once told him that when he drank, he was like a wild Indian. But to Mike, it seemed as though there was nothing else to do with his time. It was true. When Mike was drunk, he would either be chasing the girls around the bar or getting in fights. Mike wasn't considered a handsome guy and most of the girls would not give him the time of day. It wasn't hard for Mike to stir up a fight though. He was in some kind of a brawl about once a week. It was almost like a sport in Wisconsin: bar fights. Mike remembers one night he was at the bar playing foosball. He and the other guy decided to bet five dollars on the game. Mike lost the game and had to pay up. Mike needed to use the bathroom first so he walked away from the table. The other guy thought that Mike was trying to walk out on the bet so He followed Mike into the bathroom where a fight started. Mike cut his hand open on his beer glass and needed to put it on ice. The next day Mike had to go to a doctor who wanted to do surgery on his hand to repair a torn tendon. So Mike had learned that getting drunk and getting into bar room fights would cost him money.

When Mike later started working in a hospital, he noticed that the alcoholic patients were the worst patients of all. They were mean and nasty. They were dirty and unkept. If they were in the hospital for a few days they began to have delirium tremors. They would start demanding that the nurse give them their medication "right now!" The more that Mike saw of these drunkards the more he said to himself, "I never want to be like this." He also thought about how his father had wasted away so many years of his life by drinking. So Mike quit drinking and has not had a drink of alcohol in about ten years. He also stays out of bars which are nothing but trouble.

Mike also tried drugs when he was in high school. Another student sold Mike some marijuana. At that time you could get a big four-finger bag for twenty dollars. So Mike and his friends would go out into the big field behind their houses and smoke marijuana. One night all of the boys walked home from a football game together. They smoked a whole bag of marijuana on the way home. They all started laughing at each other for no apparent reason. They laughed all the way home.

Mike also tried some other drugs when they were available. One Saturday Mike and a carload of his friends went to Chicago to see a rock concert. It was an outdoor concert at Soldiers Field. When they arrived at the stadium there were all kinds of guys walking around carrying bottles filled with LSD pills. They were tiny pills called micro-dot. Mike saw blue pills, pink pills, all colors. The pills were three dollars each. Mike decided to give them a try. He bought two of the pills, swallowed them down, and found a great seat for the concert. It was a once-in-a-lifetime experience, the quadrophonic sounds of the band echoing around the field at night, Mike high on acid.

But as Mike grew older and started back in school, he didn't have time for drugs. He quit taking things that were bad for his body and bad for his mind. Besides all of the workplaces now do drug tests and a person can't even do a drug recreationally on his day off if he wants to keep his job.

Quitting cigarettes would be a more difficult task. Mike's parents both smoked. All of his adult relatives smoked. It seemed as though the whole older generation smoked. Mike remembers watching television commercials featuring different brands of cigarettes. This was a new generation of people though and people were realizing the bad health effects of smoking. Mike had been playing a lot of balls and doing some running for fitness. The more he ran the less he wanted to smoke. When he joined the Navy, he made it a goal in his life to quit smoking. He could not stop cold turkey though, that would be miserable. He also realized that whenever he had a drink, he would want a smoke so he would have to quit them both together.

Mike began to count the number of cigarettes he smoked each day. He would then go day by day trying to smoke less than the day before. At first, it was easy. Fifteen per day, fourteen per day. But as Mike reduced the number to three or four cigarettes a day it became harder. He would sometimes go outside and take a long run. The fresh air and the exercise made him not want a cigarette.

Finally, Mike got it down to one cigarette a day. He did that for almost a year before he finally quit smoking for good. Now he can't stand to be around someone who is smoking and can't tolerate the smell of a person who is smoking.

So Mike quit booze, cigarettes, and drugs. "Sometimes it is good to be a quitter," Mike said to himself.

School

If you talked to people who knew Mike when he was young none of them would have called him a good student. Most of them would have classified him as a half crazy, wild, trouble-making kid. Kind of like Andrew Jackson. Mike had quit going to high school twice. But Mike was not stupid. He had skipped a grade when he was younger. The school was easy for Mike when he put an effort into it. He was just bored after years and years of the same old thing, going to school and seeing the same people every day. Trying to keep up with the rich kids. Mike knew that he would probably end up as a factory worker like his father had. Why should he waste his time at school? Only the rich kids went to college. Only the smartest boy in the class would be a doctor is what he thought. Mike needed some parental guidance to lead him in the right direction. This he never got. His parents were divorced when he was young. He spent most of his early years taking care of himself. It wasn't until Mike became a young adult that he realized the value of formal education. It also wasn't until Mike became an adult that he started to enjoy reading books.

When Mike returned home from the Navy, he had a lot of time on his hands and he began to read a lot. He had his

GED and he had taken a college-level course. Mike decided that he would like to go to college. The University near his home had an open-door admission policy at the time. Mike went one evening with his father to listen to the Dean of the University speak. Mike remembers him saying, "This University is easy to get into but it isn't easy to stay in." So Mike took some entry-level English and mathematics classes while searching for something to major in. He still did not really know what he wanted to be. Mike also went to the gymnasium the first chance that he had.

One day when Mike was walking in the college hallway, he noticed a sign on the bulletin board that stated that they were recruiting men for the nursing program. Mike thought that nursing might be a good job in the future so he went to the admissions office and signed up for the program. For the next five years, Mike would go to nursing school and play pick-up games at the gym. College was fairly easy for Mike. He just went to class every day, listened to the instructor's speeches, and read his books. He would go to class for an hour or two and then spend the rest of the afternoon at the gym. He played against the same guys every day. He played against these guys but never thought about trying out for the team. He knew that the University had a basketball team. He sometimes read about them in the newspaper. He even knew the name of one of the players from his high school years. But Mike didn't think that he was good enough and he had to study. Even though this was a small college it was college basketball. The players were tall and they could run fast. So Mike kept going to classes, working on his grades and playing in the pick-up games.

When Mike started nursing school there were only two men in the class. When he graduated, he was the only male in his class. Mike didn't pay much attention to all of the women around him and they didn't pay much attention to him. Most of the girls already had a boyfriend and they were only interested in their studies.

Most of the classes were not hard except the physics class. Mike never liked math and he had no desire to sit in the house all night doing math homework. He knew that he needed to pass physics in order to continue in the nursing program. He did not want to quit school again. He needed to graduate from school and get a good job. He had spent most of the past few years living in a thirty-dollar-per-week apartment in the poorest part of town. Some days he ate only peanut butter and jelly sandwiches or cereal. He was happiest during these years when he had a part-time job in a restaurant because there, he could get something to eat. When he was in the fifth year of college the old car that he was driving had broken down and he spent the year riding a bus to school. A couple of times he ran all of the way home from school just to prove to himself that he could do it. It was a ten-mile run.

Then finally during his third year at the school, Mike decided to try out for the basketball team. He had been playing regularly almost every day for the past three years and he felt like he was ready. Mike had watched one of the team's games at the end of last year and he believed that he was as good as they were. So he just showed up one day at the pre-season practice and began running with the team. And boy could they run; Mike joined in a scrimmage game. He ran up and down the court so hard that he could feel his

41

own heart pounding. The six-foot eleven-inch-tall center passed the ball to Mike on the outside and Mike hit the jump shot, swish "I like that one," the center said to him.

But the next day something strange happened. Something that Mike will never forget. He had just finished a class and was walking up the hallway towards the library. Outside of the library, there was a couch where sometimes people took a break. Today as Mike walked by, he saw the whole basketball team lounging on and around the couch. They were laughing and carrying on and waiting for practice. None of them were studying. Mike avoided them. He went into the library, sat down and he began to think about it. He woke up to the reality that he probably would never play in the NBA. There were just too many good players out there. And these guys wasting their time on the couch probably were not good enough either. They would probably all just end up dropping out of school after a year or two and have to look for a job.

Mike decided right then and there that once again he would quit playing basketball and only concentrate on finishing college. It was a tough choice for Mike. He loved running and playing the game probably more than anything in life. But he also knew that it was the right decision. "Who am I kidding", he said to himself, "I need to graduate and get a good job."

When the time came for the physics examination Mike knew that he was in trouble. He had to score high on the exam to continue with his classmates. So Mike took home his physics book and started reading it from page one. He sat in his apartment for two days and nights reading that book. He did all of the practice questions and he finished the entire book. When he finished, he knew that he was ready. Mike passed the physics class and graduated from nursing school with honors. This was something of which he would always be proud of because he had not quit.

After Mike finished nursing school, he read a lot. He decided that maybe he would like to continue going to school. He had the hang of it. So he got a job working the night shift. He would try and get some exercise on his days off and he started taking classes. First, he took an extra chemistry class thinking that maybe he would like to go to anesthesia school. He enjoyed the chemistry lectures but the lab part of the class was annoying. He just went to the lab and started mixing chemicals together not really knowing what he was doing. He barely passed the lab class. But then Mike took a job in Florida. At the time there were no anesthesia schools near him so he quit that plan.

Next Mike thought about going to real estate school. Mike's uncle had worked in real estate and he had made good money. So Mike bought the books and started attending the classes. It was fairly easy schooling. One night Mike was in the class and he started thinking. Real estate commissions are seven percent of the sale. Half of that goes to the listing broker. Another half goes to the company that you work for. So if I sold a $ 100,000 house, I would maybe get $1,750. That was not very much money considering all of the time the realtor had to put in, trying to make the sale and dealing with the people. So Mike decided to quit real estate school, it was not for him.

Mike next thought that he would like to go to law school. Mike considered himself to be a good talker and a good arguer. Mike had read a lot of books, mostly history books. He had already read about Marbury vs. Madison and McCullah vs. Maryland. So he began studying to take the LSAT examination. He also checked out a few law books from the library. The law books were interesting but confusing. After reading a section Mike didn't know who had won the case. There was also a question on the LSAT that Mike could not figure out. It was a question about people sitting at a table. Some of the people did not like each other and would not sit next to each other. How would you work out the seating arrangement? Mike's answer to this was, "just sit down and shut up."

Law school was also expensive. Mike had just started working. He didn't want to spend all of his savings on law school. He had paid back his student loans and he did not want to take out another one. Besides Mike thought that there were already too many lawyers. Mike didn't want to have to compete against the others to get clients. So he quit his plan for becoming a lawyer and he never sat for the LSAT exam.

Some of the people that Mike talked to told him that he should continue with his nursing education. He should get his master's degree. Mike wasn't so sure of that. He did not like writing papers that had to have APA format. "Nursing is a women's career," Mike said. "No doctor is going to hire me to work in his office, he wants a good-looking woman around." Mike also didn't much like the idea of being the only male in the classroom. "The ladies talk and talk all day about nothing that I am interested in," he said. But he decided to give it a try. He took the master's degree entrance examination and a statistics course. Then one day he went in for an appointment to talk with the Dean of the nursing school. Mike told her the classes that he wanted to take. She looked at Mike and told him, "No these are the classes that all of the students have to take first." Mike didn't like the idea but he agreed to it. He thought that if he was paying his own money, he should be allowed to take the classes that he wanted to.

So when Mike showed up for his first day of class for his master's degree in Nursing, he wasn't happy anyway. The first hour of the class went like this. The teacher came in and said, "OK, the first thing we are going to do is sit in a circle and tell each other our names and where we are from." Mike could not believe it. "No more of this romper room stuff for me." is what he thought. So he stood up and went to the bathroom and then he exited out of the back door never to return. He quickly went over to the school admissions office and dropped the nursing class. He then enrolled in a business law class as an elective course. There he spent an enjoyable semester listening to business law lectures. He never went back to nursing school. Today when he tells his coworkers this story, he gets a laugh. His one day of master's degree school.

Work

Growing up Mike always knew that he would have to work for a living. His father and his mother both worked. Mike was not born into a rich household. Sometimes he wondered what that would have been like. Mike remembered when he was young his father worked the midnight shift at the Case tractor factory. Mike would sometimes stay up late at night with his father and eat peanut butter and jelly sandwiches. He remembers his father once telling him that if he wanted to, he could quit his job and have a job in another factory the next day. That is how many companies there were in that Wisconsin town at the time. Mike wondered how many jobs his father had really quit in his lifetime.

As soon as Mike was old enough to work, he did. His first job was as a paperboy. For this, he had given up playing football. And it turned out to be a lousy job. He had a small paper route. He didn't make any money. All of the other boys had larger routes. He had to be home every day at 4 O'clock to deliver the papers. On Sundays, he had to get up at 5 O'clock in the morning to deliver the large Sunday papers. It seemed as though all of his collected fees were going to the newspaper office. Mike soon sickened of that job and let his friend take over his route. One day they both just quit showing up to deliver papers. The manager finally just gave the job to someone else.

As mike grew older, he knew that he couldn't just keep quitting jobs. He would have to work whether he liked it or not. He had witnessed what happened to his parents when his father was out of work. Sometimes the workers at Case would go out on a wildcat strike. Mike saw how his mother would be frantically worrying if they had enough money to pay the bills.

When Mike was old enough to get a work permit, he did. He started out working in a gas station pumping gas and washing car windshields. The pay was usually minimum wage. Mike also worked in a liquor store when he was in high school. His job was to walk around dusting off the liquor bottles or to carry *a case of* beer to a customer's car. When Mike was in college he worked at a couple of different restaurants. Sometimes his job was as a dishwasher. Other times he worked as a pizza maker. He was still only making a few dollars per hour but he was also getting something to eat while working at the restaurants.

When Mike joined the Navy, he was seventeen years old. The Navy would be his highest-paying job up to that time. Even though he was the lowest paid recruit he had a place to stay and food to eat. But they kept giving him the worst, dirtiest jobs and he got sick of that. They kept giving him these jobs because he was a good worker and nobody else wanted to do them. But Mike thought that he was cut out for being better than a dishwasher. He got out of the Navy as fast as he could.

When Mike was in college, he kept working at small jobs part-time. He needed the money but it was always his goal to graduate and get a better job. When Mike started as a nurse, he worked the night shift just like his father had. Mike was happy with his work. He was finally making some money and he could live on his own. He had some time off during the day when he could play some tennis or basketball. Mike had the reputation as being a good worker. He was always on time and rarely called in sick. His patients liked him because he took good care of them. The head nurse once asked him to do some extra work sorting and filing papers. She was happy with his work. Over the years Mike just continued to do his work, putting in his time. It was almost like being a factory worker. He took care of himself and paid his bills. He was even able to save a little money.

But as time went by Mike became restless. Just like when he was in the Navy, he was being assigned the worst jobs. Whenever there was a crazy combative patient or an alcoholic patient on the unit Mike would have to take care of him. Whenever there was a 400-pound patient who could not get out of bed by himself, Mike would be assigned to them. Mike sometimes felt like he was a corrections guard or a sitter. He kept having to tell the confused patient to "stay in the bed" and to "quit pulling at your heart wires." Mike tried to talk to his head nurse about his concerns. She told him that he was given those jobs because he was good at them.

One night while Mike was having a bad night at work, he just stood there thinking to himself, "Why is it that all of my like I have been able to just quit doing the things that I love to do and yet I can't quit the things that I hate like this job?"

So as Mike got a little older, he got married and is still working. He has worked at the same place for over sixteen years. Mike's wife once asked him when he plans to retire. Every day they see commercials on the television about enjoying retirement. "I will never be able to retire," Mike said. "I will be working until the day I die, that's what people like me do." He has some good days and some bad but he knows what he has to do. He knows that every month the bills have to be paid. "The bills will keep coming in until the day I die," he said to his wife. So Mike couldn't quit working even if he wanted to.

Writing

It was probably inevitable that Mike would become a writer someday. He had an aunt who once was a reporter for the local newspaper. He had another aunt who was a grade schoolteacher. Mike remembers when he was growing up, he would frequently see his grandmother sitting in her chair with her bifocals on and reading a book.

Mike was always good at school when he wanted to be and he was good at English. Writing in school was a chore though and he wrote paragraphs and papers because he had to. Mike remembered one time in high school he had to write a descriptive paragraph. This was during his bad years when he rarely went to school. He wrote a paragraph about how lousy the school's lunches were. The teacher thought that Mike's paper was good and she decided to read it in front of the class. Mike became annoyed at this. He stood up and walked out of the English class never to return. He didn't want his homework read out loud to everybody.

Of course, when Mike was in college, he had to write papers. He did the papers that were required but he much preferred reading. There is an old saying that one is either a writer or a reader. Mike became a reader of American History and war books. He could always be seen walking around with a book under his arm. Mike even thought about becoming a History Professor. But teachers don't get paid much unless you have a Ph.D. and Mike was studying to become a nurse. But after he graduated Nursing School, he had no further desire to read Nursing books.

After college, Mike had some spare time and he tried to write a book. He was only able to write about twenty pages. Then he ran out of thoughts to write about so he quit and threw the papers away. He thought about writing a biography about George Washington or Benjamin Franklin. But there were already a million books about these guys. Almost every year a History Professor would write a book about someone that everyone had already read about. Mike wanted his book to be about something new and different. A book that might have some meaning to it. He also didn't want to feel like he was being forced to write. Like a newspaper reporter who has to meet their 500 words per day quota.

Mike kept reading his books for enjoyment but he never went back to school. After his first attempt at writing it would be many years before he attempted to write again. He stayed at the same job because he never attained higher education. He lived near a library that sold their used books and his bookshelf was filled with books up to the ceiling. If Mike was going to write again, he needed some motivation to get him started. He also knew that once he started, he couldn't quit. He was sick of being a quitter. He wanted to do something that he could be proud of.

Mike sat day after day with his pen and his paper in handwriting down his thoughts. Writing had become an obsession with him. He thought about what to write many times a day. He even carried around a small notebook to write down some of his thoughts. But when he had written about fifty pages, he began to run out of things to write about. This was the hardest part. Mike had to decide whether or not to push on and keep struggling or to just give up. He even put his writings away in the closet for a few months and took it out occasionally to read what he had written so far. "This writing isn't so easy," Mike said to himself. But he also knew that if he wanted to be good at it, he would have to work at it and dedicate himself to it. Day after day trying to achieve a higher level. Like when he had tried playing golf or playing pool.

Mike went to a nearby used bookstore a lot. One day he asked the owner if he had any books on how to get published. "Do you have some ideas for fiction writing?" the owner asked him. "Yes, I am working on it." was Mike's reply. "Well don't quit," the owner hollered. "I have known a few guys who wanted to write some music but they just stopped doing it." "I hear what you are saying," Mike replied and he just chuckled to himself.

Religion

Mike was raised as a Catholic. His grandmother was a devout churchgoer. Mike's mother made the family go to church every Sunday. Mike hated it. Sunday was one of the days that the neighborhood boys played football and Mike didn't want to miss out. He found the sermons boring and didn't understand what the priest was talking about.

Mike's mother also made him go to catechism classes once a week. Mike hated that too. Every Monday for years he was taken away from his fun and made to go to religion classes. Mike was always skeptical about the whole thing with God and Jesus. It sounded like a good story about a good man but how come nobody ever sees God? Mike was the firstborn sibling in his family. He once read a book about birth order, which mentioned that the firstborn was often skeptical. This made him feel better.

The more that Mike was forced to go to church the less he liked of it. He especially didn't like the part of the mass where you had to stand up and greet the person next to you. Someone you didn't even know. Then you were supposed to hold hands with this stranger and sing a song. Mike wanted no part of this. Mike thought that Jesus must have been a good guy. The things he taught made sense. But all of this talk about how if you sin you would go to hell and burn was a bunch of garbage. Mike knew as soon as he was old enough to quit going to church, he would, and he did.

As Mike grew older, he wondered what it would be like to be a regular churchgoer. His uncle once told him, "The older I get the more I believe in God." But Mike never went back to church and he viewed the religious pushers as phonies. In the long run, they are only after people's money is what he thought. It is better to keep quiet and to mind your own business and to work hard. The things you do in life and the way you act are more important than the beliefs you preach he thought.

Mike had a couple of friends who committed suicide. One of the boys Mike had worked with as a teenager washing dishes at a restaurant killed himself by carbon monoxide poisoning in his car. Another boy he knew shot himself in the head with a shotgun because he had lost his girlfriend. Another boy Mike knew from school was probably the smartest kid in his class every year. He attended Columbia Law School and he had a nice job for a wall street law firm. One day Mike heard from a friend that this brilliant guy who was so successful had killed himself. He had also been distraught over a woman and had taken an overdose of barbiturates.

Mike knew he would never kill himself, especially over a woman. Although Mike had some problems in his life, he felt that suicide was like quitting. Those people who Mike knew who had given up on life would never get another chance to find something new and interesting in their lives. They were the real quitters Mike thought to himself. *I don't care if I end up poor and living under a bridge, I'll just make sure I have a book to read and I'll be happy,* Mike thought. After all, the most important game was how long one lived. A person who quit something could always try something new tomorrow if he was still alive. So Mike promised himself that no matter how bad things got in his life he would not quit and waste his life away. He had learned from watching his father waste the last years of his life. There were times as he got older that he didn't think he could make it. There were times when he felt all alone. There were times when he didn't have enough money. He worried about what would happen to him and his wife in their old age. But he decided to stop worrying and live day today. He read some of his wife's books on mindfulness and being in the here and now, and other inspirational teachings. He felt better, it was almost like going to church.

Mike had a thought one day. Was it God who was telling him to quit what he was doing and move on to something else? As though he had a different purpose in mind for Mike? There are those that say that God has a purpose for everything that happens and that when a door closes God will open a new door for you. Perhaps God knew that when Mike was a grown-up, he was meant to be a worker and not a football player. Perhaps God knew that Mike wasn't really needed in the military as there was no war on at the time. Perhaps God knew that Mike was meant to be a nurse because he was a good worker whose hands could help people. Perhaps God knew the right string to pull to force Mike to quit or be removed from his task. Interesting thinking but was it all nonsense? We are all responsible for our own actions and behavior. If there is a God I wonder if he is paying attention to me. But I guess if

I wonder these things then I am still a believer. The pastor once said that God won't quit on me, so I guess I won't quit on him.

Marriage

Mike married when he was a bit older. He met a beautiful Asian girl at the restaurant that she worked at. They dated for a while mostly meeting at the bookstore or the coffee shop and they decided what the heck, let's give it a try. Mike had been a lifetime bachelor and was pretty much set in his ways. He had been in the military and he always folded his clothes and put away his things neatly. The first complaint that his wife had against him was that he was too picky. "You are always straightening and cleaning things, I can't do anything that I want to around here," she would say. Mike thought that his wife was a slob. She would leave a trail of things laying behind her wherever she went. She had purses and shoes lying about everywhere. Her dirty laundry she would just throw in a pile on the floor and leave it there for days. Mike began to wonder just what he had gotten himself into. He started doing his wife's laundry for her just to get it out of the way. Mike also hated a messy kitchen. His wife would come home at night and cook some Asian food. There was always a lot of work involved, chopping and mixing the food and a lot of dishes to clean. "It would be a lot easier just to go out to the Asian restaurant," Mike told her. "It is cheap, you don't have to spend so much time preparing it, and there are no dishes to do." This really made his wife mad as she liked working in the kitchen and preparing her own dishes.

Mike began to wonder if he should have ever gotten married at all. He told himself that he loved his wife sometimes. But there were other times that he wished that he were single again. So he could come and go as he pleased.

But quitting marriage wasn't something that a person could do easily. Mike thought about it. If he hired a lawyer that would cost a lot of money. His wife would end up taking most of what he owned. He would probably end up living at the YMCA while his wife got the house. It would be more expensive to get a divorce than to stay married. So he decided to tough it out and try and make things work.

Mike's wife also told him about the things he needs to quit. "You need to quit playing poker as all of you do is lose money." "You need to quit being so picky, and you need to quit arguing with other people," she would say. Mike heard her but didn't pay attention to what she was trying to tell him.

After a while, Mike and his wife became more used to each other. They say that the first year of marriage is the hardest. Mike began to clean the house and do the laundry when his wife was not at home. She would do most of her Asian cooking when he was at work. He would do the dishes the next day when she was out of the house. Some days they had fun when they were together. Some days they had fun when they were apart from each other and doing their own thing. When his wife went home to Thailand Mike felt relieved that he would have some time to himself. But he also missed his wife when she was not at home. Deep down Mike knew that he loved his wife very much. He wouldn't quit on their relationship. And he hoped that his wife would not quit loving him.

Pool Player

Probably one of the smartest things that Mike ever did was to quit playing pool. Pool halls are filled with bums all looking for a free handout. One thing that Mike would not tolerate was being hustled by a pool hall bum.

Mike first started playing pool when he was a kid. His father sometimes took him to the bar with him. He would give Mike a few quarters and send him to the back of the bar by the pool table. Mike learned how to hit the balls but was not a player. When Mike was old enough to go to the bar himself, he started playing more frequently on the bar tables. He became pretty good at it but there was always one or two players who could beat him.

Mike lost interest in the pool during his college years and spent all of his time playing basketball. He would occasionally play pool if he spent an evening at the bar. Mike soon began to notice however that when he went out and played pool that nobody at the bar could beat him. Some nights he would win games for hours and then lose a game on purpose just to escape the table for a while.

When Mike turned about thirty years old, he found a job in Tampa Florida and he moved there. Mike was working the night shift and on his days off he would be out playing either golf or tennis.

One day when Mike was out for lunch, he drove past a pool hall and decided to stop in. This was a big-time pool hall with nine-foot tables and a bar in the middle of the room. Mike grabbed an old house cue and started hitting some balls paying for the table by the hour. He enjoyed it right away and started practicing. This was Mike's usual method. If he took a liking to something he would practice it for hours on end. Just like when he would shoot baskets all day long or hit tennis balls against the wall all day. So Mike started to go to the pool hall every day he could and would practice all day long in the back corner of the room.

One day when Mike was hitting balls and minding his own business one of the guys who had been sitting at the bar came over to him and asked if he wanted to play some cheap games. Mike said no thanks and went back to his practice. Mike later learned that the guy who wanted to play him was named Joel and he was one of the best players in town. He was just trying to hustle Mike.

Mike had a new passion, playing pool. He would be at the pool hall hitting balls whenever he could go there. He liked the place because it was indoors out of the hot Florida sun. He did not care for the cigarette smoke or the loud music they sometimes played. Florida at that time was a gathering area for many professional pool players. Mike would sometimes watch the pros play in a weekend tournament. He even took a few lessons from them.

One Sunday Mike had the day off and he drove over to see if the pool hall was open. When he drove up to the place, he saw someone walking back and forth on the sidewalk waiting for the place to open. It was Joel. He told Mike that he had been there for hours and that he had no place to stay. Mike told Joel to get in his car. Mike then droves to a nearby hamburger place and paid for their lunches. Joel never again tried to hustle Mike after that. It made Mike stop and think though. "Is this what a great pool player looks like?" All of the pool players wanted to gamble. They all told stories about who they had beaten out of money in the past. But Mike noticed that the good players never wanted to play with each other. They always wanted an easy game. If a good road player entered the room looking for action all of the players walked away.

One of the guys that Mike played against was the son of a professional player. He had probably played pool for most of his life and he didn't have a job. Every time that Mike walked into the pool hall the kid would be sitting on a couch in the back of the room. Every time the kid spotted Mike, he would immediately come to him and ask him if he wanted to gamble on the pool. Mike would sometimes play him for five dollars a game. Mike never won. He was an easy mark. Mike didn't care though. The way he looked at it he was gaining good experience. He was going up against one of the best players in the place while the cowards were sitting and watching.

Mike kept playing pool and getting better. But he would never be anything more than a journeyman player. There were just too many good players. And Mike had a job which was more important. He could only play pool once or twice a week. Mike would go and watch a tournament and there were at least a dozen players there who were better than him. It was just like when he played basketball or golf. No matter how many hours he practiced, no matter how many buckets of balls he hit, he always ran into somebody better than him.

Mike loved to hit those balls though. The pool is an inner mental game. Mike would practice for hours by himself and feel good about his game when he was finished. He knew that he was improving. Mike never tried to hustle any of the weaker players. He felt that great athletes wanted to play against the best. To try and beat the best. But Mike kept seeing those pool players were not that way. One day Mike went to a bookstore looking for a book on pool and billiards. He found it in the store's gambling section and not the sports section.

Mike remembered an old player saying something like. "If you want to be a great pool player you have to quit your job and practically live in *a* pool hall." Mike knew that he couldn't do that. He had seen all of those basketball players standing around the couch when he was in college.

He knew that none of them ever made it big. Most of the pool players didn't work. Some were on disability. There was one guy there on veteran's disability who would limp into the pool hall using a cane. He would then throw his cane down and play pool for hours walking around the table without a problem. The guy with the cane once beat Mike a one or two ball handicap to try and win his money back. Mike wasn't worried about the small amount of money. He realized the sort of bums he was up against.

But Mike needed something to do in his spare time. Mike had basically quit playing tennis and golf because they were too expensive to play. Mike was also getting older. His days of running up and down the court were about over. But he loved playing pool, even if it was against himself. But that couldn't happen. That is part of the game, it takes two and there's always somebody trying to hustle somebody. Mike even remembered that at professional tournaments the players would be bothering each other trying to get a game to try and make some money on the side. Watching the better players preying on the weaker ones irritated Mike.

One of the players that Mike came to know a little bit was probably the best player in the area He had played for many years and owned one of the most expensive pool cues ever made. Mike often heard the guys talk about how he used to gamble. How he used to play in big tournaments. Sometimes when Mike was at the pool hall, he and some of the other players would sit and watch the guy play. He was that good. He should have been a professional. Mike knew this gentleman for almost 20 years and in all of that time never did he see the guy play a big gambling match or play in a big tournament. He always played in a cheap bar tournament against weaker players. Mike could not figure it out. He saw this great player who had all this talent and he was wasting it by beating up on lesser players. This would be his legacy. Mike wanted no part of that. That it not what any great player in any sport should be doing.

Finally a couple of times Mike lost his temper while he was playing. One day a young teenager came to Mike and asked him if he wanted to gamble. Mike took a look at the kid. He had old jeans and old shoes on and had no watch. Mike thought to himself, *"This kid probably doesn't own a car yet he wants to gamble."* Mike told the kid to get lost. Another time there were two good players in the place and Mike knew one of them. They were probably about equally matched. One of the players was itching to gamble. Mike offered to stake the player he knew $500. But he made excuses because he didn't want to play. He just wanted to keep playing against the weaker players so that he could look good. Mike started hollering at him and started calling him a wimp. "I am willing to put up the money and you don't have the courage to play him!" Mike said. He also realized that none of these guys were athletes. Basketball, tennis, golf, Mike thought that he could probably beat any of these guys at any of those games. "Perhaps you would like to play a little basketball for $500 a game!" Mike hollered at the other players. Of course nobody wanted any part of that.

Mike just kept hollering at the other players. They all thought he was crazy. But Mike didn't care. He was trying to make a point. He was sick of watching pool hall bums. No wonder that pool has the bad reputation that it has. No wonder the professional players can't make a decent living at it. Mike walked out of the pool hall and hasn't been back on one since. For Mike this was something that was easy to quit, he had experience at it.

Poker

The poker craze hit Mike when he was in his forties and living in Tampa. He remembers watching some late-night poker on the television while he was at work. He soon learned that there were a few casinos in Tampa. He began to go out to the casino on his night off. Sometimes he would stay at the casino all night and walk outside when the sun was coming up. As a night shift worker Mike was used to staying up all night.

It soon became apparent to Mike that playing hold them poker in the local games was nothing at all like what he saw on television. For starters, he would see the same players almost every time that he went to play. Everyone learned how each other played. Whether or not if they knew how to bluff. It was almost as if the same guys were just passing their money back and forth to each other. He also learned that some of the plays that worked in the high stake's tournaments didn't work in the small stakes cash game. A hand like Ace-King suited would have a television player raising or going all in. In the games that Mike played in if he raised with that hand, he would have four or five players call his bet. It then became like a Bingo game seeing which player the shuffling machine would give the good cards to.

Mike never did trust the shuffling machines. *Any machine that is run by a computer chip has to be rigged*, Mike thought.

Mike soon started losing money like most of the players do. But he kept going to the casino late at night because it was open late and there was nothing else to do. Most of the players were known as nits. They were hit-and-run players. They would sit and play for a while usually buying in for the minimum amount. As soon as they won one or two hands they would get up and leave with their winnings. Of course, this was legal. But it wasn't a real poker game. Another player who was losing would have to sit there for hours trying to get his money back. But he couldn't because the nits had left and taken most of the chips with them. As soon as the losers were even, they too would leave the table if they were smart. It was hard to win at this game.

Mike often became tired of losing money at Poker and he would quit going to the casino for a while. He once quit going for more than a year. But then he would be at home with nothing to do so he would venture out to the casino for something to do. He never really has been able to quit this entirely. But he thinks to himself that if he only goes once in a while and is not hooked on gambling it is the next best thing to being able to quit entirely.

Other Pursuits

Mike briefly tried many other things throughout his life but he quit them all. He would try something new, become interested in it for a while, and then move on to something else. It seemed as though Mike was good at many things. But he would never be great at one thing. Mike tried out for the Junior High School gymnastics team and actually competed in a few meets. He had a friend who was into gymnastics and Mike decided to give it a try. Mike soon learned that he did not have what it takes to be a gymnast. What is required is good arm strength. Mike was stronger in the legs; he soon gave up on gymnastics.

Mike even tried some springboard diving. He had some experience at cliff diving as there was an old rock quarry in his hometown that had filled in with water. All of the boys would go there and jump off of the cliffs. A few boys drowned there. Mike wasn't much of a swimmer. Some days he just liked to jump in the pool after playing some basketball just to cool off. But one year just for kicks he tried out for the High School diving team. Once again, he had a friend who was on the team and he drove Mike to the practices. Mike was a diver, not a swimmer. He had never practiced swimming. He had never swum more than a lap in the pool. The swim team swam laps twice a day, before and after school. Then one day at an interschool meet the coach tells Mike that he was putting him in a swim relay race. Mike was supposed to swim four laps in the pool. Mike had never before swum four laps in his life. But Mike didn't argue with the coach and he did what he was told. He swam as best he could but by the third lap, he was tired out. His muscles became so tired he could hardly move. He almost drowned. Mike barely finished the race and that was his last day on the diving team. The coach called Mike into his office and told him that he was kicked off of the team. The coach said that students who smoked cigarettes could not be on the team. Mike really didn't mind, he just said "OK," and left the room. He went back out into the gym and played some basketball. But later Mike thought long and hard about what he should have said to the swimming coach. "Any coach that puts a person into competition without that person having a chance to practice and prepare has no business being a coach." And Mike knew what he was talking about. He had seen better coaches and had been on better teams. So here was an instance where Mike didn't quit but wasn't upset when he was no longer on the team.

Mike also tried playing the trumpet for a while. He liked to listen to jazz music late at night. He started collecting old jazz records and spent a lot of money on them. He liked reading the back of the album covers which contained some good histories of the bands. So Mike tried for a few months blowing on the trumpet, never having taken a lesson. But it gave him and his neighbors a terrible headache and it was noisy. He sold the trumpet at a pawn shop. He still listens to jazz records with his headphones on.

Tampa has a large Hispanic population. One night Mike went out and stopped at a bar in the neighborhood. There he saw people salsa dancing and he became interested. Mike started going out once a week on Latin night to dance and see the women. He didn't drink alcohol and mostly stood around watching. He enjoyed looking at the Spanish ladies but of course, they wouldn't have anything to do with Mike because he was white and he couldn't dance. So Mike decided to take some dance lessons. He found a married couple who were the best dancers at the place and they gave lessons. First, he took some group lessons and learned the basics. But Mike in his usual enthusiasm wanted to be better. A dancer is like an athlete Mike thought, and he wanted to be good at what he was doing. So Mike started taking private lessons from the couple once a week. He took private lessons for more than a year and he became a pretty good dancer.

Now some of the ladies saw that Mike knew how to dance so they would dance with him. Mike even took a weekend trip to Puerto Rico to check out the salsa clubs, He went to a local bar there and none of the ladies would dance with him. He stood there all night watching.

But Mike started to develop a sore knee from dancing. It is a common problem among dancers. His coach had to have knee surgery once. He saw a woman at the bar and she said she had three knee surgeries. Mike talked to an orthopedic doctor who told him, "The only way to stop your sore knee is to quit dancing." So that is what Mike did.

Anger

Mike had problems with anger ever since he was young. He was frequently getting into fights at school. He became sensitive to criticism and short-tempered. If someone called him a weakling or a slow runner he would soon be involved in a fistfight.

The fights that Mike was involved in when he was younger are not like the fights of today. They were basically fistfights with a circle of boys standing around watching. Usually after a few minutes, one of the boys would gain control by getting his opponent in a headlock and the fight would end. Mike even remembers fighting with someone and giving him a black eye. The next day that same boy walked up to Mike laughing and wanting to make friends. "Look at what you did to my eye," he said while holding out his hand in friendship. It is nothing like the fights of today where someone will pull out a gun and start shooting over a small disagreement.

As he grew older Mike was still quick-tempered and sensitive but he knew that he could not just use his fists every time he became angry with someone. But Mike was annoyed when he walked out of the poker room after losing money. He was angry after leaving the pool hall after being harassed by hustlers. It seemed that he was angry all of the time. So Mike realized that he needed to find a way to quit being angry. His wife once told him, "You argue with everybody." And it was true. Mike didn't like his neighbors. He didn't like his neighbor's dogs. He didn't like many of the people that he worked with. He didn't like Florida because it was too hot. He often wished that he could just quit his job, sell his house and leave without leaving a forwarding address.

Mike was becoming a miserable person and he needed to find a way to become happy. He finally decided to get some professional help and he started going to anger management meetings. There he listened while some of the others talked about their problems in their relationships. He learned a few things at those meetings. He also started reading books about anger management and spirituality. This was one way that Mike learned the best and felt the most comfortable, by reading. He learned that getting rid of anger problems takes time and practice. A person who is angry needs to work every day all day at not become overly angry. Anger was something that Mike would not be able to quit overnight.

So Mike tried to spend his time doing the things that made him happy like reading and taking long walks in the evening by himself. He also tried to avoid the things that made him unhappy like arguing with people every time they said something that he didn't like. He stayed away from bars and pool halls. Now Mike likes to think that he is becoming less of an angry person. He waves hello to his neighbors when they are walking their dogs. "It is good practice,"

Mike says to himself. "If I am going to quit being angry, I am going to have to give it some effort."

Regrets

Almost everyone will tell you that you should never quit. Quitters never prosper. As Mike grew older and became aware of how many times, he had quit something, he wanted to know why. Was it an inner habit? Did he believe like his father that if he quit something he could easily go on to something else? Did he repeatedly quit because he knew that he wasn't good enough? Did he quit because he wanted to save himself the embarrassment of being kicked off of the team? Did he quit because he became tired of trying to achieve that higher level that he thought he would never attain? Or was he just bored with what he was doing? Was Mike just a loser?

Mike didn't consider himself a loser. He had played on three championship teams in his youth. He had played football against bigger and tougher boys and had earned their respect. He could play a game of golf and shoot in the high 70s. He once did a high dive off of the highest cliff at the swimming quarry in his hometown. He had graduated college with honors. Mike felt that he had many great life experiences as well as failures.

When Mike played pool, he had played against the best. He didn't try and hustle the weaker players. The best players came to him because they knew that Mike would give them a hard-fought, honest game. Trying all of those different sports made Mike healthy. On any given day he could do what he wanted to. If it was raining outside, he could go and play poker or shoot some pool. If it was a nice day outside, he could go and play some golf or some tennis. If he felt like going out at night he could go and do some salsa dancing.

Mike never attained stardom in any one thing and he regretted that. He never did pursue any one thing for the length of time that is required for greatness. He often wonders what would have happened had he stuck to only one thing like football. *Football players are making millions of dollars and I am working my tail off just to pay the bills,* Mike thought. And the reason that some of the players at the pool hall were so good is because that is all that they did for their entire life, practically living in the pool hall.

But Mike also knew when it was time to quit something. He knew what his priorities in life were; work, marriage. He also knew that it was good to quit something that was harmful to yourself like smoking or drinking. He knew he would never have made it in the NBA. Mike occasionally watches games on the television these days and he thinks to himself, *I was better than some of these players, I know a dozen players that were better than these guys.* Mike had learned quickly that he wasn't cut out to be a lawyer or a gymnast and he quit those pursuits right away. He also knew when he needed to quit playing pool. He didn't have the temperament for it. The bar atmosphere and the daily battles against other players wore on Mike's nerves. He realized he started becoming annoyed or losing his temper that it was time to quit. He couldn't afford to get in any fights. He figured that sooner or later he would find something else that he was good at that really moved him. He hoped that he would find a new passion.

Mike had learned other things from quitting. He knew that there were important things in life like marriage and work that a person should not give up on easily. He had learned that sometimes if you quit it is hard to go back and start over. The memories of how good you once were at something make it hard to climb the achievement ladder again.

So Mike accepted the fact that he was a quitter. But he also liked to think of the accomplishments he had obtained in life. He had married a fine woman and he had worked in a job for many years where he was helping people. He was still healthy and happy and free to do anything that he wanted to on a given day. He went to the bookstore on his day off. He took his wife out to dinner often. He went to the poker room once in a while. He took long walks in the evening to relax. He even sat down and tried to write a bit of something.

CPSIA information can be obtained
at www.ICGtesting.com
Printed in the USA
LVHW081222310523
748422LV00009B/109

9 781685 623302